"I thoroughly enjoyed this book. The truth is that you have a mi[...] when you understand how to use it effectively, you can create anything you desire in your life."

—Peggy McColl
New York Times Bestselling Author

"Christine has expressed her knowledge and understanding of higher mental faculties which are an essential key to our growth and expanding conscious awareness. To provide so much value of how the human brain works and how we can create results that we desire from early ages with ease has been long needed subject to feed all minds. Christine beautifully demonstrates to young minds how connecting to your inner power can unleash your unlimited potential. Learn how to develop the faith in yourself and believe that you can achieve anything. Nothing is impossible. I absolutely love this book and would love to see it in every young generation's hands."

—Vladimira Kuna
International Bestselling Author of *The Bible of the Masterminds*
Enlightenment and Mindset Mentor

"Children will be excited to learn about their own power, when they unlock their hidden treasure, the six intellectual gifts found within. These compelling messages can stimulate the mind and enable better decision making, which foster balanced perspectives on life. When practiced, these lessons never grow old and evolve as they mature."

—Nicki Cunningham
Designer, Writer, and Composer of the *Daily Dose*® song, in support of optimizing mental health and wellness initiatives.

"This book *Magic Thoughts in Your Mind* is a brilliant explanation of how you have within YOU all the power to create a life you love. And the approach is simple enough, anyone can apply it. I recommend everyone add this book to their personal library. Definitely a gem of inspiration and profound education. Hats off to the author Christine Lee!"

—Gregg Hammond
Author, Musician, Mentor, and Founder and President of the Global Jam 4 Peace

A MESSAGE FROM
Bob Proctor

Dear Christine:

I want to congratulate you for believing in yourself … for taking control of your life.

It doesn't seem all that long ago when I made a similar decision and I've never looked back. Sure, there were days when I felt as if I couldn't bear to learn one more lesson … and I still have those days and will continue to have them, but I've learned that they're a necessary part of the process. You see, I don't believe we just wake up one day and "*get it*" … understanding is not a destination. Awareness better prepares us for what's next … and when we've learned all that we can on that particular frequency of life, we move up to a higher frequency.

When you began this journey with me and my team, you had the desire to make a positive change in your life. And because of that desire and commitment you made to yourself … you risked, you remained committed, you took action, you challenged yourself and you ultimately grew … by a quantum leap. Maybe it was in your thinking … or your income … or the relationships you've built with those closest to you. The improvement or change may be glaringly evident in some areas, even actualized by the attainment of a specific goal … in other areas of your life the change may be more subtle – but rest assured, it's there. One thing is true and that is you have brought more of yourself to light. By **being** more, **doing** more, and **having** more … you're creating a better world for those closest to you and the rippling effect will impact others you may never meet.

I congratulate you on your decision to live a fuller, richer, and more abundant life. It is vitally important that you continue to do in the future what you've been doing over the past year … organized study with a specific objective in mind – to create a greater awareness. I remember the exact date I completed my first year of structured and assisted study – October 21st, 1962. I remember it because my coach, Raymond Stanford, invited me to his home to congratulate me on what I had achieved and stressed the importance of making this form of planned study a priority in my life. I took his advice seriously and I encourage you to do the same.

Don't forget the commitment you honored and the growth you attained by seeing this program through to the end. Celebrate your achievement – you are one of very few people in the entire world who made and then lived into such an extraordinary commitment in the pursuit of excellence as an individual and as a beautiful and unique expression of spirit.

It would be easy to sit back and rest, thinking you have completed something. Reflect on your achievements, but continue on your journey … even kick it up a notch! Be true to your commitment … keep learning, keep searching, and continue to reach for the stars.

Make every year better than the last!

Sincerely,

Bob Proctor

MAGIC THOUGHTS
in your MIND

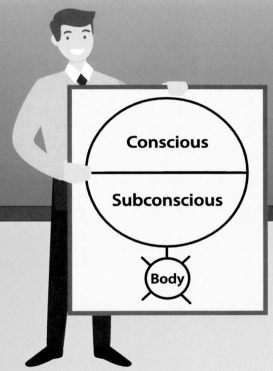

CHRISTINE LEE

Hasmark
PUBLISHING
INTERNATIONAL

Editor: Stephen Buffey

Cover and Interior: Anne Karklins
anne@hasmarkpublishing.com

ISBN 13: 978-1-77482-135-0
ISBN 10: 1774821354

This book is dedicated to all the children and unborn babies.

*And to my role models and mentors Bob Proctor and Peggy McColl.
It is because of their dedication that so many lives can strive to
be more, do more, and have more.*

FOREWORD

In writing this book, Christine has moved beyond labels placed on us by our parents, our teachers, and society in general to say what she came to see is the heart of a well-lived life. In her own journey, and in her books, she has chiseled away at the biases we all grow up with. In this book, she takes us to what's of real value, which is how the human brain works, how we can affect the way it works, and as a result live a higher quality life.

From a young age, Christine has never been able to simply say what people are used to hearing or wish she would say. In so much of her life, she goes beyond the mindset of the world as we know it, taking us into a place that few on the planet have so far explored. She introduces us to what her life has taught her through all of her many experiences, as well as with help from those who have walked this path before her.

This book will teach you things beyond what you know—certainly beyond what the world around you knows. Like her first book, this is a book that on a different level asks us to push past fear, judgement, and negativity of every kind. Christine has learned to embrace the idea that her lived experience can change the lives of many.

Growing up, Christine was gradually able to trust in herself. She found a path that is unique to her, and in this book she invites her readers to do the same. In this tutorial of the mind, she focuses on the different parts of the brain, showing us how they are designed to all operate together. If anyone has had to use their imagination and intuition, Christine is a powerful example of how these work in everyday life.

You will realize that, rightly understood and used, your brain is not here to trick you, but rather it can enable you to become the special person you are meant to be, and how to be guided from within. You will no longer miss out on the deep connections that life invites you to take advantage of. You'll learn to function at a soul level, with the body and the mind in perfect rhythm.

As Christine was able to identify the gifts her mother gave her, you'll learn to appreciate your own background, so that you become a light to the world around you. Greatness is yours—it's just a question of going beyond what's holding you back.

—David Robert Ord, Editor and Ghostwriter

HELLO, HI! IT'S ME, YOUR BRAIN, THE AREA THAT MAKES ALL THE DECISIONS FOR YOU.

The one that decides if you like a certain food or want to play a particular sport. I'm the one that sees your friends doing something and says, yes, I like that too. The one that plays video games all night with you and knows that this decision is right no matter what your parents have said.

What I am specifically talking about is your Mind. Your Mind has an incredible power to guide you through life automatically. It helps you make decisions so you can have as much fun with your friends, have a loving relationship with your parents (even though sometimes it doesn't feel like that), and grow up to be whatever it is you want to be.

What if I told you that your Mind has a magical power that you can control and make decisions for yourself and have the best life you can think of, that you can dream of, and it all starts with YOU!

We live in a world with so much going on around us. You get up in the morning, have your breakfast and get ready for school. You're in school all day using your brain and Mind, learning and receiving all the information your teachers tell you. Then it's home time, and you may have after-school sports, other activities like music, gymnastics, or dance, then homework before dinner and bedtime. Then you repeat it all the next day.

Like I said, a lot going on!

As you get older, your responsibilities change, you become the one making the decisions on how to spend your day. What courses do you want to take in high school?

What after-school activities do you want to continue? And maybe you're the one helping decide and cook what's for dinner.

Using your Mind's magical powers all starts with the practice of understanding how your Mind works. This will help guide you to make the best decisions for your life when you choose those courses in high school and when you grow up to decide how your life will turn out.

So, what are these magical powers you keep hearing about? They are the six gift faculties:

1) **IMAGINATION**
2) **INTUITION**
3) **WILL**
4) **MEMORY**
5) **REASON**
6) **PERCEPTION**

But wait, what does *faculties* mean? It is an ability to do something or create something using your Mind. An example of this would be having the ability to make new friends easily, or having the potential to go really far in dance if you put your mind to it.

Let's jump in and start learning about how your life can change just by using your Mind!

CHAPTER 1
UNDERSTANDING THE MIND FIRST

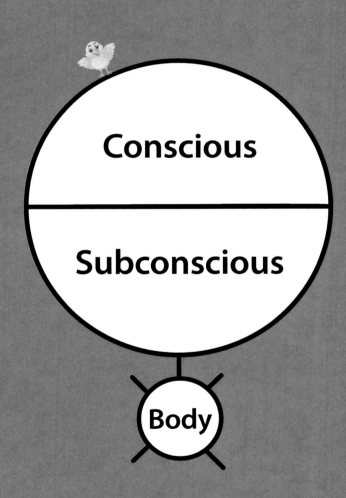

UNDERSTANDING WHAT ALL THIS MEANS is the first step to achieving this greatness. A man named Bob Proctor uses these pictures called The Stickperson to help explain what is going on in your Mind.

These pictures help show how your Mind works by using your imagination to pretend the pictures are your Mind.

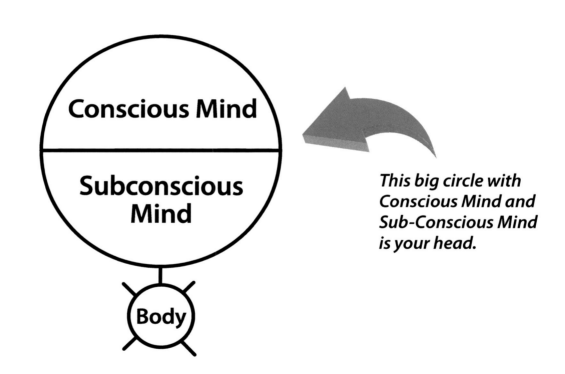

This big circle with Conscious Mind and Sub-Conscious Mind is your head.

WHAT DOES CONSCIOUS MIND MEAN?

It is everything you think of while you are awake. It creates memories of the fun things you are doing right now. It helps you understand your feelings and your wishes and helps you choose what you want to do now and later.

WHAT DOES SUB-CONSCIOUS MIND MEAN?

It is the most powerful part of your Mind. It is the part that remembers and believes what your conscious Mind has decided on. It is also the part that stores those memories that you created and brings them out when you want to think about them. It helps your beliefs come true. Whatever you think (good or bad) your sub-conscious will make it happen.

Your *Conscious Mind*, the top half of your head, pulls information from all different areas of your life, and this is how you form your thoughts, feelings, and decisions. You have influences all around you that help make these decisions:

- family
- friends
- teachers
- coaches
- the radio
- television
- video games
- social media

These are all part of your daily life and influence your thoughts and choices, also creating what you like and dislike in your life.

Your **Subconscious Mind**, the bottom half of your head, can hold on to more information than you can dream of. It will remind you how you feel about something.

Your **Body** is all of you. It is the total package all together from your Conscious Mind to Your Subconscious Mind. The thoughts you choose every day makes up the thoughts you always go back to even when you're not thinking about them. Your Body is what makes it happen.

Let's pretend that after only a few lessons, your conscious Mind has decided that you don't like math, and it is really hard. All of a sudden, your subconscious Mind agrees with you and every time you are in math class, you think, *"I'm never going to get this. It's a waste of time, and I don't understand it anyway."*

What you are doing is allowing your subconscious to keep believing this way.

Now let's see if we changed this around a little. Let's pretend that after only a few lessons, your conscious Mind has decided that this math is taking a little longer to understand, but you like it and will keep working on it until you fully understand. Now your subconscious Mind agrees with you, and every time you are in math class, instead you think, *"Wow, this is getting easier the more I practice it; I think I am getting faster at working on the problem and maybe I can start learning the next step."* Now, what you are doing allows your subconscious to believe in yourself and what you can accomplish.

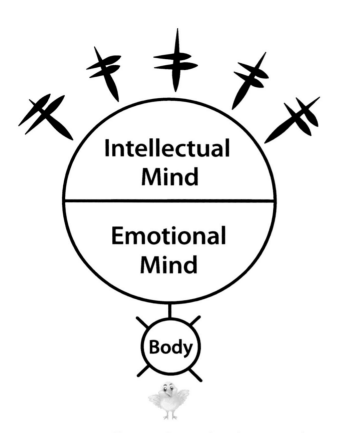

Your **Intellectual Mind** is the way you choose to think. It is the 6 gift faculties.

1) IMAGINATION
2) INTUITION
3) WILL
4) MEMORY
5) REASON
6) PERCEPTION

Your **Emotional Mind** is how your thoughts make you feel. They are your 5 senses.

1) SIGHT
2) HEARING
3) SMELL
4) TASTE
5) TOUCH

Your *Intellectual Mind* is the part that makes you think about everything. It is the area that helps you understand right from wrong and helps you remember and learn new things in school and other areas of your life. This part of your brain is what you will use to make daily decisions now and as you grow up.

The *Emotional Mind* is how you feel about what is happening around you. This is where your five senses come into action.

When we use all of this together, it becomes a pattern in our daily life. You start with your thoughts, which turn into your feelings that become an action you take and then become your results.

It is up to you how the result will be from the very beginning. If you want a better outcome, then you will have to start by changing your thoughts.

Let's go back to the math example. In the first thought, the decision was made that math is hard and you will never understand it, which resulted in you not liking math and thinking you would never understand it. But in the second thought, you changed your mind to believe you would understand it and it would just take a little longer to learn. This result ended more positively because you changed your thought in the beginning to believe you could do it.

Going through life will always be about how you're going to see a problem (good or bad) and think how am I going to solve it. Using your six gift faculties will always help you achieve a more wonderful life because you think clearly and positively about the outcome. No matter how challenging it looks at the start.

You want the magical thoughts in your Mind to be turned into the results you want.

It's time to start understanding how to be happy, joyful, successful and get everything you can dream of out of a life you will love.

CHAPTER 2
GIFT FACULTY #1 – IMAGINATION

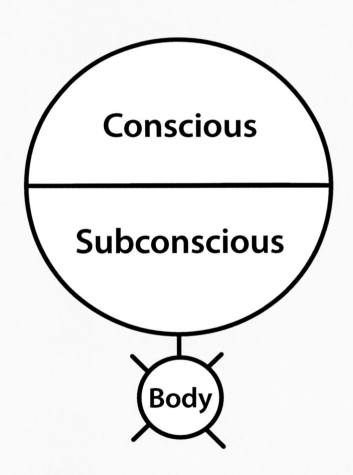

HELLO, MY NAME IS IMAGINATION, and I can be anything your Mind can create. I am your ideas and dreams that you think about or act out when you're playing, drawing, or pretending to be somewhere else.

Imagination is the beginning of every creation. Someone imagined the house you are living in before it was built, and a clothing designer imagined the clothes you wear every day before it was made and sent to the store where you bought it.

Imagine: It's time to go on vacation, and you can go anywhere you want. Tell me:

- Where will you go?
- Who will you see?
- What will you eat?

You can create anything you want when you use your Mind. It's like your brain has its own superpower, and it can build anything you want without touching it. When you spend time using your imagination, you're planning what you want to do in your life now. When you grow up, all the things you imagined can come true.

Imagine: You just woke up in your favorite drawing surrounded by the best colors and the most awesome things around you. What do you see?

Let's see what Johnny imagined:

Instead of watching TV one day after school, Johnny found himself sitting in the backyard on a big green and brown checkered blanket with his dog Lucky by his side. His blanket was so soft and warm that it made him feel like he was lying on the sand with the sun shining down on him surrounded by clear, warm light-blue water and tall palm trees with coconuts. Johnny loves the beach and would love to be there every day. *"One day, I will live on the beach,"* he imagines, *"and have a boat so Lucky, and I can go fishing. I will live in a blue house because blue is my favorite color and have a helicopter to take me around."*

Johnny awoke from his daydream and quickly went inside to draw this image he had created in his Mind. *"I am going to put this picture on my wall so I can look at it every day and see where I am going to live when I grow up."*

Imagination can take you to places you can only dream of and build the best day ever in your Mind. You can design buildings and clothes, a new toy or even create the first-ever … I don't know, you tell me!

Be sure to tell your parents about all the beautiful dreams and creations you think about, and one day it could come true.

Anything is possible if you use your imagination.

IMAGINATION

CHAPTER 3
GIFT FACULTY #2 – INTUITION

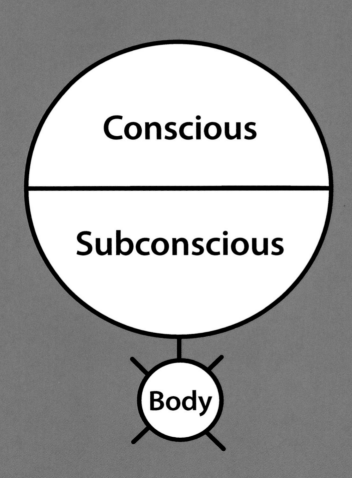

HI, MY NAME IS INTUITION, and I'm that feeling you sometimes get deep down in your stomach that tells you this may not be the right thing to do, or that there is something special you are passionate about, like drawing or dancing and would like to do it every day.

Intuition is sometimes the best way to understand what is really important to you at that exact minute.

We don't always listen to our Intuition because our Mind tells us otherwise. Sometimes we don't listen because we are so busy playing or talking to or texting our friends. And sometimes, we ignore our gut entirely because we want to fit in and do things our Intuition tells us not to do.

Imagine you are on a walk with a friend along a beautiful trail in the woods. You see a path with sunflowers and butterflies, the sun is shining, lighting up the way, and then you look to your right and see trees and a dark path with branches covering most of the walkway.

What path is your Intuition telling you to take?

It may be exciting to see what's down the shady tree-lined path, but your gut or Intuition tells you not to go that route. Listening to your Intuition is like a spiritual guide giving you the information you need to make decisions.

Another way to use your Intuition is by understanding what the person next to you is feeling without them even saying a word. This is known as picking up the energy that they are giving off. Have you ever seen someone extremely happy, and all of a sudden you feel much happier just by being around them? Your Intuition is reading their energy and becoming part of how you feel.

It's important to listen to your Intuition or inner wisdom to help you solve a problem you are facing or discover something new about yourself. Remember to write down what you have discovered, as you never know when you may need to hear it again!

Madison was walking home from school one day with her friends, listening to one of them talk about how she did on her spelling test in class that day. The friend explained what words were on the test and that she had forgotten how to spell some of them. Madison started helping her friend with some of the words she didn't remember how to spell because she felt that her friend was looking for help at that moment. It was then that Madison realized that she likes helping people, especially when it comes to schoolwork and thought, *"Maybe I could be a teacher one day."*

CHAPTER 4
GIFT FACULTY #3 — WILL

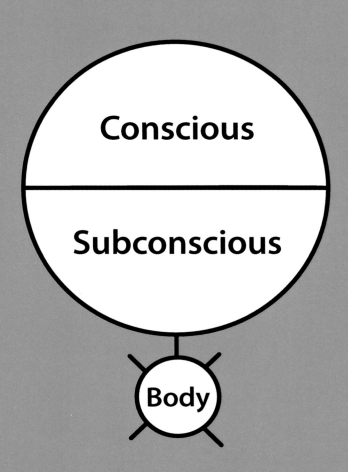

HI, MY NAME IS WILL or, as some call me, **Willpower**. I am the part of your magical Mind that can be stubborn and determined, the part that wants to get exactly what I'm looking for.

If you're going to be the best basketball player or dancer and are just new to the sport, you will have to create the Will to learn and be better at it. This may mean you are up before school starts to practice with your coach, as well as practice a little in the evening to get where you want to be.

Willpower takes a lot of concentration and practice but can be applied to anything in life. You can even use your Willpower to save your money for a trip you always wanted. The Will tells you not to spend your money right away but to save it for that very special trip or thing you have always wanted.

Imagine you saw the most fantastic bike you have ever seen while at the store. This bike was very expensive, and your parents said you could not have it. All you do is think about this bike, dream about it, and know it will be yours one day. But how? You know you get money from doing chores or other jobs, so you think this is how I will save up for this bike.

Willpower is about thinking of how you will accomplish the task of getting your bike and the discipline you need to save money. There is a saying, "If there is a will, there is a way," and that, along with discipline, will allow you to save the money to get the bike of your dreams.

Willpower is great to start practicing now because it will be easier to use as you get older. If you take one idea and focus on that without any other distractions from your five senses (sight, sound, smell, taste, and touch), you are working on your ability to concentrate, making your thoughts much more powerful. Practicing this can help you in every way, from your homework to sports, to reading and even when you think who you want to become!

Once you learn this skill, you can apply it to anything! The world is yours!

Johnny was frustrated that he kept running out of time to do his homework, practice basketball, eat dinner, and have time to hang out with his best friend after school. He didn't like getting in trouble with his parents. After all, Johnny left his homework to the last minute because everything else was more important to him. He sat down and took a good look at why he didn't have enough time for everything when he got home. Johnny realized a pattern that was happening when he arrived home from school: he watched TV ... not just a little, but almost from the time he got home until it was dinner. He made the decision to concentrate on changing this pattern so he would have more time to have fun with his best friend later.

Johnny decided to use his willpower and commit to coming home from school and completing his homework while he has a snack. This way, he could practice basketball right before dinner and then hang out with his best friend before it was time to go in for the night.

Johnny soon realized that if he could use his willpower to make this change now, this would help him as he grows up and has to accomplish more in a day.

CHAPTER 5
GIFT FACULTY #4 – MEMORY

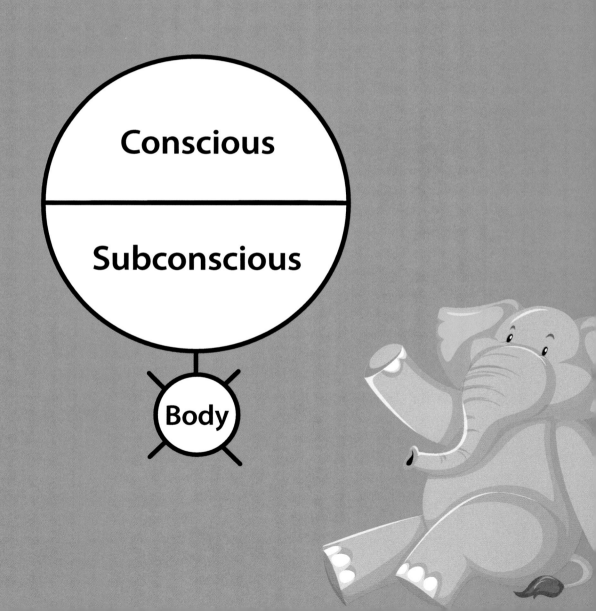

HI, MY NAME IS MEMORY, and some people feel that I am not that strong in your Mind and I forget everything, but that's not true. I am as good as you believe I am.

It's important to practice me all the time as I will improve the more you work on me.

Memory is a very magical part of your life because it's the ability to remember all the good and even bad times in your life. Good memories can make us happy, and bad ones can help us learn what not to do next time or what powerful message there is to be discovered.

The more we remember, the richer our lives are.

Do you remember that time when you went to that exciting place you had never been to before? Tell me what it was like?

Now, do you remember the music that was playing? The food you ate? The smells all around you?

That sounds like a great memory!

The best way to develop a stronger memory is to pay attention to one or all of your five senses (sight, sound, smell, taste and touch) when you're in every situation. This will help trigger the thought or memory in the future. An example of this would be if you hear a song that has just came on the radio and it reminds you of the time you were dancing with your grandma in her kitchen. It just brought back a happy memory, and it was because of the sounds. Now, if you remember what she was cooking in the kitchen and what plates you were going to set the table with, you have included three senses to your memory to help you remember it further.

It was a cool, fall morning and Madison was walking her usual route through the pathway at the end of her street on the way to school. As she neared the end of the path, Madison entered the small forest that was the beginning of the school grounds. But something was different this morning. The air had the smell of a real fireplace in the distance, and it was almost like the trees had changed color overnight. It immediately made her think of when she was smaller, and her dad would rake the leaves so she and her brother could jump in, and then later they would go inside for hot chocolate by the fire. This was such a great memory and gave Madison a cozy warm feeling that would be with her for the rest of the day and maybe ask her dad to rake some leaves when she gets home from school!

CHAPTER 6
GIFT FACULTY #5 - REASON

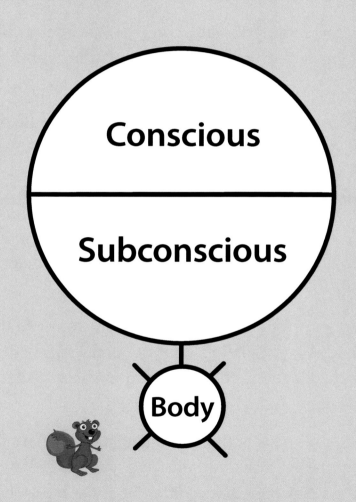

HI, MY NAME IS REASON, and I am the part of your Mind that helps you think things through. If done right, it helps you make good decisions that will set you up for success now and as you grow up. If you come to a place in your life where you just don't know what to do, the reasoning starts to happen and you allows you to talk it out in your Mind and decide the best possible outcome for this situation.

Reason is your greatest tool, and it allows you to think about what you want now and later in life. It is also there to help you understand and think about the situation that just occurred.

Think of a time when you were so excited to play with your friends who were waiting across the street, and you just ran to meet them. Once you got there, you realized that you didn't look both ways before you ran across. At that moment, you realized you weren't thinking.

You often hear an adults say, "Listen to reason." There is an important message in this, as with Reason comes a clear mind to help you understand what is really happening at that moment.

Applying reason to your thoughts is also like brainstorming. It can be as simple as listening to a friend's idea and building on it or coming up with an entirely different thought based on the first idea. The best part about reason is that any new thought or idea can be part of the strategy, no matter how big the idea.

Johnny was sitting at his desk at home thinking about what had happened in class that afternoon. He was paired with another student and they had to work on a project together. Johnny and his classmate had a different opinion on what the project should be, and they had a disagreement. He was upset that his ideas were not taken seriously and thought, *"We can't do this project together, it's never going to work out."* The longer he sat at his desk, he started to think about what his partner's ideas were. *"Maybe it wasn't so bad,"* he thought, *"we can take both our ideas and combine them to create a great project."* Johnny started to think of more ideas and went back to school to discuss them with his partner. They came up with a plan based on adding more ideas that started with their original brainstorming ideas. Johnny realized that the longer he sat and thought about his problem, the more he could figure out a solution and think of new and exciting ways to fix his problem.

CHAPTER 7
GIFT FACULTY #6 – PERCEPTION

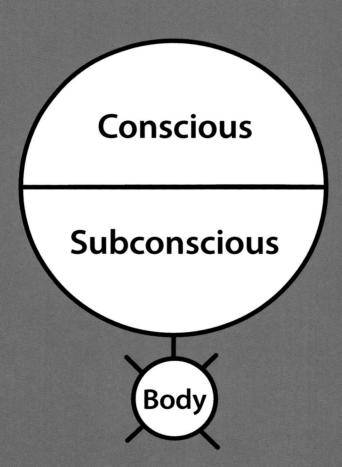

One of my favorite quotes by Wayne Dyer is,
"When you change the way you look at things, the things you look at change."

HI, MY NAME IS PERSPECTIVE, and I am how you see things.

I am that area of your Mind that decides how something happened and then believes it to be true. I have the ability to shift my Perspective, but I need your help.

Have you ever looked at something and thought, *"it wouldn't help me"*? *"I will never be able to use it and leave it there for a while."* Then one day, you walk past it and think, *"this may help me out."* That is changing your Perspective!

When you change how you see yourself, your everyday thoughts and how you talk to yourself change. You realize you have the power to become anything you want. Thinking positively and living with a positive Perspective can help you live a life you only dreamed of.

If you see yourself as having less than a friend you aspire to be like, changing your Perspective will help. Why not decide that you not only have what they have, but you have more. You have the best personality, the best outlook because you're so friendly and kind. The best wardrobe because it's for you!

Again, when you change the way you look at things, the things you look at change!

When you look at something the same way each time, you are not helping yourself to grow. Once you decide to see something differently, you start to realize that you have the power in your Mind to change the outcome. It may be that you don't like the way your bedroom looks and you keep telling your parents that you need to change it. The paint color is all wrong and your furniture is not your style. But then one day, you see the sun shining, highlighting a wall, and you think, *"If I add this poster and a few pictures to this wall, then the color will go perfectly. If I move my dresser to another area and my bed to another wall, I will have more space to move around."* You may discover that artwork you are proud of should be framed and displayed in your room, making all the difference.

Perspective is challenging how you understand something to be true and look at it from a different angle. It has the ability to change your life for the better, it's all a matter of how you view it!

Madison is on the track team at school because she loves to run and was asked by her coach to join the relay team, where she would be part of a group that runs together. Immediately she thought, *"I am not good enough to be part of this team, I can't run fast enough and what if I made a mistake."* Madison's Perspective is that she would fail and couldn't do it. She had self-doubt. The coach asked her to come to a practice to see how she felt and if it would be a good fit. Madison explained that she didn't think she was good enough to be on the team, and maybe she shouldn't go. The coach explained that she was a fantastic runner, and she just had to see herself the same way he did. Madison went home that night thinking about what the coach had said. Soon after, she thought, *"I love running and have been pretty good at it on my own. I will go tomorrow and show the team how fast I can be."* This made Madison feel better about herself and the decision to be part of the relay team. Changing the way you see yourself and the way you think can make all the difference. Believe in yourself just as others do, and you will see just how far you can go!

CONCLUSION

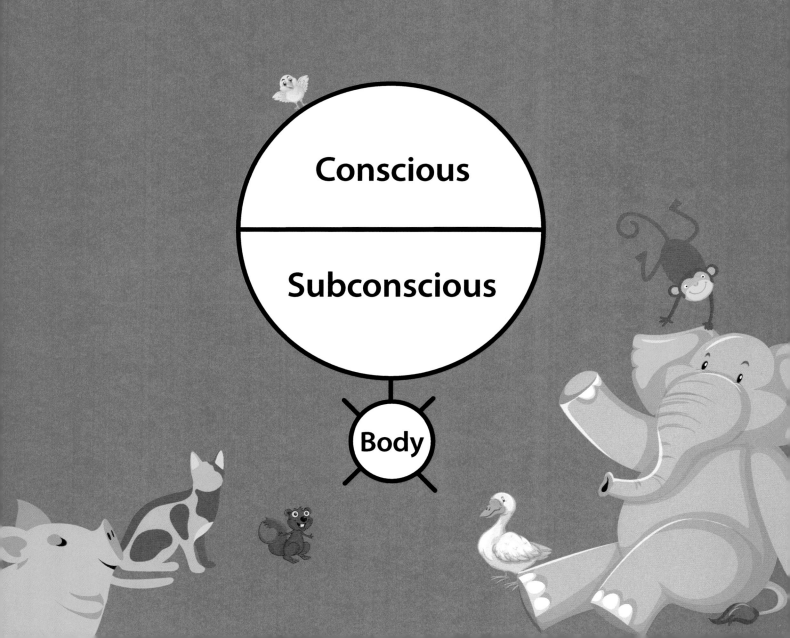

OH, HI! IT'S ME, YOUR BRAIN AGAIN, OR SHOULD I SAY YOUR MIND.

The part of you that was born to stand out from the crowd and let you be exactly who you want to be.

The six gift faculties taught you to think from the inside out, using your **Imagination** first to create the ultimate life you want now and for your future. Your **Will** helps you concentrate and focus on achieving what you imagined for your life. Your **Intuition** will help guide you along the right path and pull you back when you feel you're going off track.

Don't forget about your **Memory**, which holds the key to past lessons, joys, and reminders of how good life can be. It reminds us to see the good in everything and live life to the fullest.

Living the life you want allows you to show up every day, excited for what is to come. With the good, there is always the bad, and that's where your **Perspective** is important. Look at everything from a different view and apply **Reason** to discover the best possible and positive outcome you can.

YOU have the power to create your own world no matter where you are starting from.

YOU are the one that is in charge of your thoughts.

YOU are the one that can make your dreams come true by using the Magical Thoughts in your Mind!

THE END

Christine is an entrepreneur, educator, and Destiny Property Coach.

Christine has led a very colorful life and relies heavily on legacy, culture, and history to assist her in her thought process. A third culture woman from Korea, Christine moved to the United States when she was a child. The deep part of her roots and upbringing has led her to many different parts of the world.

As a mentee of Bob Proctor's teachings, Christine follows a very simple law, which is the law of attraction. Her success has been guided by Bob's masterful teachings and has opened a pathway for her to write her debut book, *My Hero – A Love Letter to my Mother*. Her life was transformed when she registered for one of Bob's monumental events in LA, titled the "Science of Getting." Mesmerized by the experience, Christine embarked on a journey to invest in herself to become part of his elite circle. Since 2014, Christine has put Bob's teaching at the forefront of her mind to create a life of abundance and success. He visited her school campus during that year and inspired her colleagues and students on practices geared towards a life full of prosperity, abundance, and serenity.

In her latest book, Christine reflects on the teachings that have had such a profound impact on her life, and hopes she can play a part in helping the next younger generation live their most fulfilling and authentic life.

For more information about the author, please visit:

www.christinerlee.com

Facebook: Christine Lee

LinkedIn: Christine Lee

Or email: inyekim@gmail.com

HEARTS to be HEARD™

Giving a Voice to Creativity!

With every donation, a voice will be given to
the creativity that lies within the hearts of
our children living with diverse challenges.

By making this difference, children that may
not have been given the opportunity to have their
Heart Heard will have the freedom to create
beautiful works of art and musical creations.

Donate by visiting

HeartstobeHeard.com

We thank you.